D1308426

If The Trees Could Talk...

Written by Stuart A. Kallen

Illustrated by Kristen Copham

SLOATSBURG PUBLIC LIBRARY
1 LIBERTY ROCK RD
SLOATSBURG, NEW YORK 10974

Published by Abdo & Daughters, 6535 Cecilia Circle, Edina, Minnesota 55439.

Library bound edition distributed by Rockbottom Books, Pentagon Tower, P.O. Box 36036, Minneapolis, Minnesota 55435.

Copyright ©1993 by Abdo Consulting Group, Inc., Pentagon Tower, P.O. Box 36036, Minneapolis, Minnesota 55435. International copyrights reserved in all countries. No part of this book may be reproduced without written permission from the copyright holder. Printed in the U.S.A.

Edited by Julie Berg

Library of Congress Cataloging-in-Publication Data

Kallen, Stuart A., 1955-
    If the trees could talk / written by Stuart A. Kallen
        p.   cm. -- (Target earth)
    Includes index.
    Summary: A tree talks about how it was planted and the important part it plays in the environment.
    ISBN 1-56239-184-4
    1. Trees -- Juvenile literature.   [1. Trees.   2. Ecology.]
I. Title.   II. Series.
QK475.8.K34   1993
582.16 -- dc20   93-18991
                                     CIP
                                     AC

The Target Earth Earthmobile Scientific Advisory Board

Joseph Breunig—Curriculum Integration Specialist at the Breck School, Minneapolis.
Beth Passi—Education Specialist; Director of the Blake Lower School, Minneapolis.
Joseph Reymann—Chairman of the Science Department at St. Thomas Academy, St. Paul.
Larry Wade—Scientist-in-Residence for the Hennepin County School District, Minneapolis.

Thanks To The Trees From Which This Recycled Paper Was First Made.

Abdo & Daughters
Minneapolis

If The Trees Could Talk...

They would say...

Leaf through the pages of this book and learn.

Listen to the words of the world's smartest tree.

We promise you won't be left out on a limb.

A warm and gentle wind is blowing today. My leaves are rustling in the breeze. It's a great day to be a tree.

In this forest, from where I grow on this hill, I've seen a lot since I was a tiny *sapling*.

At one time, Native Americans lived beneath my leafy green canopy.

Today, I can see highways, malls, and suburbs growing closer every day.

Sometimes I get scared and wonder if someone will cut me down. But today I'm happy just to be me—a tree.

Day by day, and inch by inch, I have grown up more than 30 feet (9 meters) into the sky.

Winter, summer, fall, and spring, I am all the things a tree must be.

My branches are a home for owls, chickadees, and cardinals. My mossy trunk is a home for caterpillars, hornets and ladybugs.

My roots drink water and keep the soil from washing away.

y leaves make food for me to eat and air for you to breathe.

All creatures, large and small, need trees like me to stay alive.

At one time I was just a seed among thousands of others that fell to the ground. I am a sugar maple tree. My seed was on a "whirly-bird" that helped me fly away from the tree that made me. I "helicoptered" to the spot where I am now growing. That was a long time ago.

For a while, I was just a skinny little sapling, struggling to grow tall. The taller I grew, more sunlight hit my leaves.

My leaves take *carbon dioxide* from the air and mix it with water gathered from my roots. When this happens I produce *oxygen*. This process is called *photosynthesis*. That's a big word, but if you say it like four words, you can learn to say it right. Photo. Sin. The. Sis. Photosynthesis!

Carbon dioxide is the gas you exhale when you breathe "out." Oxygen is the air you breathe "in." Humans and animals exhale carbon dioxide and inhale oxygen. Trees inhale carbon dioxide through their leaves, and then exhale oxygen during photosynthesis. Pretty neat, huh?

cientists say that without trees, the world would have too much carbon dioxide and not enough oxygen. Carbon dioxide is a gas that is making the Earth become too warm. You might have heard people talking about *global warming* or the greenhouse effect.

Some scientists say that if the Earth gets too warm, the climate will change. It might get so warm that palm trees could grow in a cold place like New York! Now everyone likes palm trees, but if it gets too warm, all sorts of bad things can happen.

The ice at the *North Pole* will melt. That will cause water to rise and drown out cities by the oceans.

It might also turn places that grow most of our food into deserts where nothing will grow.

ow that's pretty scary. But you can help—take it from me—a tree.

You can help by planting trees and saving the forests where they grow.

Eco – Activities

1 Watch a show on public television (PBS) about forests and rainforests. Look at a listing of television shows, like the *TV Guide*, and find a show you think you might like. Pay close attention to the parts of the show that talk about global warming and the cutting down of forests.

2 Look at the trees that grow where you live and find out what their seeds look like. Oak trees make acorns. Maple trees make "whirlybird" seeds. Pine trees make pine cones. Plant a seed indoors and watch the tree grow. When the tree is big enough, plant it outdoors where it can grow into a big tree.

3 Ask a parent to take you to a park where many trees grow. Notice the many different plants, seedlings, and trees. Gather leaves of different trees and make drawings of their shapes.

4 Paper is made from trees. Recycle newspapers to help save trees. Ask your school and parents to recycle paper.

5 Cars add to the greenhouse effect. Try not to use the car as much. Walk, ride a bike, or take the bus. Ask your parents to drive less.

6 Hug a tree!

E_{co} – F_{acts}

BAD NEWS: It takes 500,000 trees to supply Americans with their Sunday newspapers every week.

THAT'S A LOT OF FORESTS: Americans use 850 million trees *every year!* The wood is used for building, boxes, paper, and many other things.

SAVE THE RAINFORESTS: Fifty acres (20 hectares) of rainforests are cut down every minute of every day. That's 27 million acres (11 million hectares) a year, an area the size of Ohio.

BAG IT: It takes one 20-year-old tree to make only 700 paper bags. Refuse bags at the store or recycle the bags you take. Ask your parents to bring cloth bags from home to use at the grocery store.

GOOD NEWS: New lumber products have been developed out of recycled wood. These new products can be used as material for building houses, saving thousands of acres of old growth forests.

Glossary

Carbon Dioxide - A colorless, odorless gas. Carbon dioxide is formed when things burn or decay. The burning of oil, coal, wood, and other fuels releases carbon dioxide into the air. Plants use carbon dioxide during photosynthesis.

Desert - A region without water and trees.

Global Warming - Also called the greenhouse effect. Global warming is caused by too much carbon dioxide in the air. Global warming could cause the Earth to heat up.

North Pole - The northern end of the Earth's axis.

Oxygen - The air we breathe. Trees produce oxygen during photosynthesis.

Photosynthesis - The process in which trees take carbon dioxide from the air, mix it with water, and produce oxygen. This process feeds the tree.

Sapling - A young tree.

Write or Call

American Forest Council
1250 Connecticut Ave. NW
Washington, DC 20036
202-463-2455

Global Releaf
P.O. Box 2000
Washington DC 20013
202-667-3300

Nature Conservancy
1815 N. Lynn St.
Arlington, VA 22209
703-841-5300

The Rainforest Action Network
301 Broadway
Suite A
San Francisco, CA 94113
415-398-4404

TARGET EARTH™ COMMITMENT

At Target, we're committed to the environment. We show this commitment not only through our own internal efforts but also through the programs we sponsor in the communities where we do business.

Our commitment to children and the environment began when we became the Founding International Sponsor for Kids for Saving Earth, a non-profit environmental organization for kids. We helped launch the program in 1989 and supported its growth to three-quarters of a million club members in just three years.

Our commitment to children's environmental education led to the development of an environmental curriculum called Target Earth™, aimed at getting kids involved in their education and in their world.

In addition, we worked with Abdo & Daughters Publishing to develop the Target Earth™ Earthmobile, an environmental science library on wheels that can be used in libraries, or rolled from classroom to classroom.

Target believes that the children are our future and the future of our planet. Through education, they will save the world!

Minneapolis-based Target Stores is an upscale discount department store chain of 517 stores in 33 states coast-to-coast, and is the largest division of Dayton Hudson Corporation, one of the nation's leading retailers.